further
TRANSPORTS OF DELIGHT

SPIKE MILLIGAN'S
further
TRANSPORTS OF DELIGHT
MORE AMAZING REVOLUTIONS

Photographs by Popperfoto

Sidgwick & Jackson London

First published in Great Britain in 1985 .
by Sidgwick & Jackson Limited

Copyright © 1985 Spike Milligan (text)
Copyright © 1985 Popperfoto (photographs)

ISBN 0–283–99274–3

Designed by Paul Watkins
Phototypeset by Falcon Graphic Art Ltd
Wallington, Surrey
Printed in Great Britain by R.J. Acford,
Industrial Estate, Chichester, Sussex
for Sidgwick & Jackson Limited
1 Tavistock Chambers, Bloomsbury Way
London WC1A 2SG

Foreword

The success of the previous volume *Transports of Delight* has caused Sidgwick & Jackson to squander the entire profits, which reached three figures, on a second sale-shattering sequel. The resignation of the entire board of directors is just a coincidence, as it was with the first volume.

Comforted by this, a Mr Spine Milligan has been approached to write the sequel. Doing business through a letter-box was a hindrance, but he finally agreed, and within these mute pages is what he deems his finest 'middle green period' work.

Signed

Jack Hobbs,
Vagrant and pianist.

The publisher on tour, accompanied by his bodyguard and soothsayers.

Note

Since the stunning success of *Transports of Delight*, where eighty-nine copies were sold in one month, I have been researching the further methods by which man transported himself, and likewise made his transport safe and, of course, durable over long distances. The best example and the ultimate refinement of this is the Concorde aeroplane. Bearing in mind that it still cannot take off or land without the most ancient of perambulators, the wheel, it would be otiose to suggest that without primitive man's invention the Concorde is a failure, but the fact is that it is so; but I digress.

From the beginning of time, things had to be taken from A to B; OK, but when you had to get to C D or E and finally Z the limits of endurance were reached. In passing I may refer to the Victorian era of travel, when great explorers/travellers like Livingstone only got reported when they had reached the 'limits of their endurance'; until you reached that, the Royal Geographical Society were not interested in you. The other way to fame was to 'discover' something like the Victoria Falls 'found' by Livingstone; they had in fact been there all the time, known in Bantu as 'The-Great-Cloud-of-Water-that-Thunders-and-Keeps-All-Bloody-Awake-at-Night'.

Methods of long-distance travel were imperative to such explorers, the greatest distance being covered by Decimus Burton (famous for his having gone on a search for the source of the Nile). (HP and Lea and Perrins were another two.) Despite the steam engine and the steam boat and the steamed envelope, all Victorian explorers were dependent on the Coloured Gentlemen, or Blackamoors or niggers (from Niger – hence the word nigger); as there were no steam-propelled niggers, these poor Africans had to carry, paddle, push, pull all the explorers' vital equipment for 'discovering' the mighty Zambesi. A mile-long stretch of porters could be seen carrying gas stoves, pneumatic beds, portable ballroom tents, ice-making machines, mahogany cupboards, silver dinner-services, Broadwood grand pianos, zinc-lined butterfly nets and brass malaria-proof Souzaphones; all this paraphernalia helped fill the letters that cleft-stick runners bore home.

Burton wrote:

Hungagoli, April, 1871

Dearest,
Have just dined in the desperate jungle circumstances, my leech-picker took three off the piano leg as I played Schubert's 'Ich heim ein shatzen mit ein'; the silk on the inside of the dining tent is wet with the jungle evening mist, thank God for the 40 ton gas-fired coal fire that warms the interior. Alas, the pâté de foie gras has fallen victim to salmonella and we dined on quinced mottles from Fortnums . . . soon thank God I will be between my monogrammed sheets and blacking out the Hell that this place is.

I will write again as soon as I've shot another elephant in my pyjamas.

Yours ever,
Decimus

This then was what real travel was made up of. He forgot to mention that 200 of his niggers had been (a) eaten by lions, (b) slain by tribesmen, (c) drowned, (d) poisoned by pâté de foie gras, or (e) killed by him. But it is thanks to men like him that we can now beat an easy path to one-time inaccessible parts of Africa, where we are loathed by the inhabitants.

Exploring was really travel with adventure, and the possibility of a knighthood.

In recent times the late Orde Wingate was seized with the peculiar English fever of venturing into the desolate sandy wastes of the Arabias (he was also a distant relative of Lawrence of Arabia). Yes, he took himself two camels with aught but dates and water-containers and set off on a desperate journey to go it alone from Souk el Kemis (just outside somewhere or other) to the legendary Siwa Oasis, in whose pursuit a legion of Alexander's Infantry had vanished, starting the 'Lost Legion Legend' or was it the 'Lost Legend Legion' or the 'Legion of the Lost Legend'? Whatever, he set off dressed as a Prince of the Desert, lean, learned and loony. For fourteen days and nights he trekked doggedly, having to eat one of his camels on the way, before it ate him. He finally, after a month, arrived at the Oasis, only to discover that there was already a regular bus service there every hour. It ended his thirst for travel adventure in the classic Islamic mode; he then opted to teach the Jews how to shoot the Palestinian Arabs, a remarkable change of heart.

Another peculiarity in the travel world was American.

1. Howard Hughes

The tycoon of American air travel was Howard Hughes. This extraordinary mammary-orientated American was born in a safe deposit along with a billion dollars in loose cash, which he inherited. His burning desire was to leave his stamp on the world; it started with a series of round-the-world air flights wearing a trilby hat, as against Charles Lindberg in his Spirit of St Louis, who, even though the plane's cockpit was enclosed, insisted on wearing the leather 'Biggles' flying helmet and goggles first made popular by Ben Lyon in the film *Wings*. Howard Hughes by doing it in a trilby hat upped his ratings in the Macho Man stakes.

He flew around the world in all directions, including both, always wearing the trilby hat and a Clark Gable moustache. He next travelled towards Jane Russell's bosom; she was a nobody when he met her and he promised her, after several legover situations,

that she'd soon be very big in films. He invented a special bra for her: technicians worked through the night to have the bra in position for the next day's shooting; they fitted the bra, and then he realized that despite it all she still only had two. What has this got to do with travel, I say; my dear reader, I have asked Howard Hughes that many times, and do you know what, it foxed him too. However, running parallel with this bra venture his airline was covering the whole of America. Then one night God spoke to him: why not fly the *whole* of America to England, Paris, Vienna?

He set to with nothing but $10 billion to design a giant seaplane; the rest is history. It was the Spruce Goose, made entirely of wood and money. People laughed at Christopher Columbus and then at Howard Hughes. 'It'll never fly,' said Glen Miller, who knew a thing or two about planes but not enough. 'I tell you this plane will fly America to London,' said Howard Hughes. The first trial flight was on the something or other in 1940; he took the controls of Spruce Goose, and made it fly 13 feet above the water for 8 minutes. He landed with a trilby hat and a Clark Gable moustache. 'I told you so,' he said, then rushed to a wash-hand basin and washed his hands seventy times with a trilby hat on. It was another world record, and the start of a mania about dust-borne disease that made him fear to leave the confines of his airtight plastic sack, in which he sat with his money, being fed through sterile tubes. He never ventured forth again.

2. Wilhiem Schatzhaus

Oberleutnant Wilhiem Schatzhaus transported a giant steam-operated engine to German East Africa; with it he hoped to open up the jungle to 'civilization'. The huge machine was assembled at Hertzstadt on the African coast. The giant All Iron Steam Traction Engine was blessed by a Pastor Einpiesporter, the troops of the Imperial German Army fired a salute, the German flag was hoisted, the band played 'Deutschland Uber Alles'.

'Feirwartz!' shouted the Oberleutnant. Driver Schnelenbalz threw the combustion handle, released the brake, great chuffs of black smoke enveloped the crowd, steam hissed through ladies' legs causing disturbances and children were blown backwards by the blast. The whole giant machine shuddered and shook, started to glow red-hot, then exploded. So there, another travel adventure written off.

3. Larrington Moonrash

This extraordinary man was a lay preacher: he could only preach laying down, due to his having lost a leg in the First World War. He was seized with the idea that he could be the first one-legged man to ski across Canada from east to west to raise money for one-legged charities. He was sponsored by the Laidlaw and Pills Leather Truss Company, whose condition was they would put up £10,000 for his trip, but he would have to wear one of their leather trusses *outside* his trousers. At first the Reverend Moonrash objected, but then they showed him the money and he was very moved and agreed to wear the truss. It was his undoing: the leather truss is made to be worn between two legs, and alas he was one short. However, he set off from Vermont in a snowstorm with the truss in place; within 5 miles it ruptured him, and the great attempt was over. He sued Laidlaw and Pills, who settled out of court in oncers, but oh bitter pill – for the rest of his life he had to wear one of their leather trusses.

4. Mark Holworth

Mark Holworth was the instigator of the most daring travelling stunt ever conceived: he was to cross the Niagara Falls in a gas stove and go down the convolution of the Niagara River into Lake Spikious. The gas stove was upholstered to avoid any damage during the journey. It was waterproofed by the Canadian Army and tested underwater in a Navy Depth Tank, where a Navy diver lived for two days. All set, then, on the Sunday, Holworth – wearing pneumatic clothes – entered the gas stove, and it was cast off a launch above the falls where it sank like a plummet. He had forgotten to close the door.

5. Miesu Louis Crute

He was born in Nice, his father being Theo Crute the famous entomologist, who was researching the amazing relation of strength to body weight of insects. For instance, Crute Sr discovered that ten stag beetles could pull a Wellington Boot, that a fly could lift up a cigarette end, and that ants supersede all other insects as being the true Herculeses of the insect world. One bull driver ant actually pulled a jam doughnut on a special trolley across a room! This so excited Crute Jr that when he grew up he made a special sand sledge and announced to the world that he would harness a million driver ants to it, then, by holding a stick with ant attraction food on it as bait, make the insects pull him across the Sahara. Camp was set up at Tizi Ouzu on the lip of the Sahara. In a special container were one million ants; Louis Crute slept in his solo tent. On the morrow he and his Arab boys would set to harnessing the ants; for this he had made special protective anti-formic acid clothing. Alas, during the night the ants ate their way out of the container; they also ate the Arab boys and Louis Crute, a cruel blow to the world of transport.

6. Heriot Merton Bentine

This adventurer/traveller is obsessed with the polarity of travel; he knows that the North and South Poles have been discovered, but he is also positive that no one has found the East or West Pole. Next year, with the backing of a rich homosexual pop millionaire, he is setting out with an ice-breaker moored at the Thames and four sets of husky dogs; the world awaits.

7. Patrick O'Looney

Intrigued by Thor Heyerdahl's success in using reed boats made in Egypt to cross the Southern Atlantic and prove that the Egyptians could have been the ancient Aztecs, O'Looney made a raft of potatoes with the intention of navigating it to Egypt to prove that the Irish had built the pyramids.

With nearly two million spuds stitched together, he launched himself into Dublin Harbour and was given a great send-off by a man called Tomas. Thanks to exceptionally good weather, he navigated the Bay of Biscay, entered the Straits of Gibraltar, and sailed into the Mediterranean, where it was high summer and the sea water hot. So hot it boiled the potatoes and most of them flaked away. The rest were eaten by fish. With only four potatoes left, he lost his balance and had to swim for it. Thus his attempt failed; however, the Pope congratulated him on being a Catholic.

8. Lopez de Tonne

In 1900, inflamed by the increased use of the submarine, this rich Bayonne fur merchant put all his money into building a submarine for discovering the 'hidden world'. The craft was made by the now extinct Grille Maritime Company of Marseilles. Lopez de Tonne manned it with an ex-French Navy crew, a Captain Maurice le Delte in command; he took many bottles of champagne on board to celebrate places that he would find hidden under the sea. They set off with little publicity, the submarine named Violetta after his mistress, who sailed with him and who, despite the protests of the Captain, took her dog Peta, a small thing with hair on. The orders to the Captain were 'Go to Africa, submerge, discover the bottom half'. It could never work:

there were no underwater viewing ports. Nevertheless, this was not realized until they finally reached the coast of Dahomey; from then on they could only find land on the surface, and this had already been discovered. By now the barking, defecating dog had driven Captain le Delte to the point of insanity. In shark-infested waters he tried to throw the dog overboard, a hand-to-hand struggle twixt de Tonne and le Delte ensued, the submarine was docked, the Captain was fired, and le Tonne and Violetta settled in the Port of Gondo in a small missionary settlement, awaiting a new captain for their return. One never came. De Tonne, Violetta and her dog were eaten by cannibals. To this day the submarine lies rusting on the beach.

A GLC publicity stunt.

9. Mungo Park

Yes, Mungo Park, childhood hero of Branwell Brontë, was yet another of those Englishmen who thought that various parts of Africa should be found/investigated/mapped/navigated/logged/measured/discovered. In 1803, this early exploring loony was exploring the upper reaches of the Niger, and according to the *London Gazette* of 15 May 1804 had 'brought the interior of Africa to the notice of the public'. Like the rest of the steely-eyed derring-do jutting-jawed Anglo-Saxons, with plentiful financial backing from friends, societies, city guilds, he did it all on the backs of the poor blacks while he strode in front with a walking stick, but he was not alone. Africa was alive with these 'I must be first to find' nutters, among them dashing Major Denham and *his*

walking stick, who was discovering northern and central Africa. Going across this line of travel was yet another, Sir John Ross, his pipe and *his* walking stick; not far away carrying *his* walking stick in a south-eastern 'I must find the middle of Africa' tour was William Edward Parry. Then there was the Reverend Richard Trevelyan, who was obsessed with teaching 'the black woeful heathen' the ways of the Lord, and distributing knickers and bras in Xhosha Land. There were dozens more 'I-must-find-it-first-for-my-country' loonies. They suffered no more than their poor black porters, but if they were taken with a fever, it appeared in *The Times*: 'Gallant English Explorer Leonard Twit Stricken with Swamp Fever', while the deaths of their poor carriers were ignored. It was all great fun, the supplies of niggers seemed endless.

One peculiarity: whenever they 'discovered' a waterfall, it was immediately named either Victoria or Albert Falls; to this day Africa is littered with minor Victoria Falls and Albert Gorges, oh what bliss to find one called Mrs Aida Biddles Falls, but then she didn't dish out OBEs. It was an age when white men 'opened up Africa', and look what they found. Do not let these stories deter you from continuing the History of English Adventurers – there are still interiors waiting to be opened up; as I speak expeditions are trying to find their way out of the Barbican.

THE NON-RETURNABLE SEAPLANE

Originally called the Icantsee plane, this was
due to the very retarded position of the pilo
cockpit, and it has a devilish history. T'
pilot was Dick Scratcher, who wa'
affair with Sheena Motts, wife o
Howard Hughes designer Lennar
swore secret revenge on Scratche
his time. One day as he was biding,
Hughes – from inside a hygienic see-t
anti-agent orange bag – asked him to α
new seaplane. Knowing that the test pilo
would be Dick Scratcher, Lennard Motts
designed a devil of a plane, the cockpit we
back down the fuselage. After the plane too
off the front part of the plane suddenly starte
to stretch and increase in length so that Dick
Scratcher's vision was totally obscured;
consequently he and Mrs Motts (who
accompanied him) were never seen again. The
photograph shows the plane as the front part
started to stretch.

**Right: The plane Motts designed in case Dick
Scratcher came back.**

**During prolonged traffic delays, a lorry driven by Mick Docherty
finding its own way out of the Blackwall Tunnel.**

LONG GERMAN BIKE. TOO MUCH TOO SOON In 1984 Herr and Frau Krikke had been trying to have a child for eighteen years without success. They consulted the famous Hindu gynaecologist Fakri Rantooli. He administered a fertility drug under strict controlled supervision and nine months later Frau Krikke gave birth to thirty-five boys and one girl. When they were of a perambulating age, Herr Krikke invented this multiple fertility *fammillienbike*. Here we see the family out for a Sunday spin *en route* to lunch at the YMCA. Herr Krikke is not with them. He is in prison for murdering Dr Rantooli.

This shows the Gerstdachen Police mounted on a bike they use to pursue and arrest the Krikke family for speeding, as they often do, reaching speeds of up to 100 miles an hour.

A French restaurant sinking.

Advancing soldiers having just been hit by porridge.

In the *Guinness Book of Records*, the world's unluckiest man is listed as Ali Ben Narkers of Medjez el Bab in Tunisia. In 1984 he bought a camel to transport his heavy load of dates to market across the Sahara Desert where rich profits were to be had in Timbuktu. Alas he discovered that the camel had Sponks disease – a rare camel illness, the animal in question being permanently thirsty. To suffice its thirst you have to travel with a 1,000 gallon tank; this keeps the animal from collapsing.

This is the Knutts-Mosley family. Keen gardeners, in the autumn they planted 2 million crocii, and we see them here in the early spring trying to avoid them.

In Ponkello, Italy, a narrow-gauge railway bridge collapsed over a dry water-course. Estimates to rebuild the railway crossing varied from £1 million to £800,000. However, a late tender from Mick Looney and Company said they could do it for £3 10s and a box of carrots. This is Mick Looney showing the completed railway crossings.

THE OVERLAND MARALINGA HOUSE RACE

This takes place in the dry season in Maralinga, Northern Australia, when the water dries up. Bathing is prohibited, and then when things become unbearable the position of the nearest water-hole is flashed on the news. The houses line up, a cannon is fired and the great house water-hunt race is on. Here we see Bluey Cobblers crossing the finishing line.

This unique photo shows the great camel carriage and white pony collision in Bombay in 1889. The white topied man is the Governor-General Lord Campbell-Wellington, on his way to take tea with the Maharani of Bophal who, through confusion, was on her way to have tiffin with a Major Victor Trebelis, who used to do things to her. A third party mounted on a small white mountain pony was Miss Jessica Cronwalis-Crapton who was on her way to any place she could make the damn thing stop. Alas, these three transported people were travelling in the *karawan*, a heavy mist caused by the overheating of stale curry. As this was an anniversary of Krishnu, the god of overheated curry, there was a profusion of this mist, and it was in these crepuscular circumstances that the three parties collided at speed. Owing to the *karawan* curry mist, no one could see, so they shouted at each other until the mist rose, when this enterprising photographer caught a once-in-a-lifetime shot of India under the Raj.

THE EFFECTS OF RATE-CAPPING These are people of the village of Bowder in the Chilterns. Their local council were against rate-capping and over-spent their annual budget so they were totally skint. Dramatic cuts had to be made: first to go were the trains, then the buses; this left them with bullock-hauled sledges. Here we see a number 329 bullock sledge on its way to Reading.

o opinions: (a) the horse has
ted to choose which one fits.
the man dressed as Napoleon.
he horse; the case continues.

THE IRISH HYDROBIKE This bike is for crossing shallow fords. The bike is collected at the bank of the stream, then the passenger runs quickly with it to the other side, where he discards it, leaving it ready for a return crossing. The beauty of this bike is you don't have to ride it.

The photo taken over Tara airfield a moment after the tragedy. Th[is]
passenger plane commissioned by Aer Lingus, newly formed in 1929. T[...]
off with a full load of twenty passengers, who were treated to a cha[...]
aboard; it was during this lunch that a fault in the linking bolting went [...]
whole floor and the sides of the plane fell off. It was not until they stopp[...]
planes of cardboard and leather that the airline prospered[...]

This photo has baffled analysts the world over. There are tw[...]
just let off, or (b) they are training it to fly; the reader is invi[...]
Note the elastic reins which had dreadful repercussions on [...]
Another opinion was that the man let off and frightened t[...]

This is the amazing *SS Doris*, named after its owner, Mrs SS Doris. She had inherited a vast fortune from her father, who made underwear for perverts and sold it by mail order. When he died he left her £1 million in cash and 20,000 pairs of crutchless black silk knickers. She longed for a sea voyage, but alas suffered *mal de mer* and sea-sickness, so the *SS Doris* was built in a quiet backwater, suspended between two supporting pylon walls fixed to the sea bed. This way Mrs SS Doris spent many happy weeks aboard her ship. To give the effect of the ship travelling around the world, every week the crew was changed for a different nationality, likewise the cuisine.

A quaint custom in Partujo in the Algarve in Portugal. On 23 March they all take their cypress bushes for a walk and sing songs to them as they go, drinking liberally from their wine carafinoes. At sunset the bushes are replanted and the entire village is arrested for drunkenness.

REDRUTH, CORNWALL At a caravan site overlooking the sea, special hides are made for those people who are ashamed of their older-type horse-drawn caravans. These hide-a-car sheets are rented out to the impoverished owners, in this case so humiliated by their appearance that they fled from their two scruffy canvas seats, seen in the foreground. The owner of the caravan is believed to be Lord Lucan.

For many years the search for the composer of 'Roll out the Barrel', sung by both armies in the Second World War, has continued. The composer was finally tracked down to a beach in Spain; he has never received a penny for the song.

A Zulu houseboy, outside the office of the *Natal Courier*, claiming to have just flown the Atlantic by winged rickshaw. Unfortunately no one saw him do it.

OUDNDATTA, NORTHERN TERRITORY, AUSTRALIA Tom Daft, an alcoholic ploughman, so addicted that he was forced to tow this 1,000 gallon beer-tank to help him 'top up' when ploughing. It took him three months to plough a one-acre field. He does not get much work.

A LET OFF FOR AMERICA When the Zeppelin 'Hindenburg' flew over New York in 1937, Hitler was already preparing for war. This flight, in fact, was a trial run for a German Pearl Harbor, and the German Captain Von Hizenuf was mapping every building for destruction. At that time Ronald Reagan was a B-movie cowboy, who later went on to be a B-movie president. When he saw the Zeppelin for the first time, he said 'Gee Whizz'.

Mr Len Grotts sees the result of the new 'car reducer' on his Ford Capri. This new method of making the car smaller was essential because his garage was not large enough. However, with the new 'car reducer' the Capri now fits snugly in the corner.

TEXAS, USA A unique moment in the Presidency of the United States. A present from the citizens of Brownsville, a solid gold railway carriage made for President Ronald Reagan, intended to be used during his 'delusions of grandeur you ain't-seen-nuttin-yet' period. The truck is shunted to a quiet layby near the prairie; here he takes all his clothes off and screams for several hours. The turbanned brown devil under the buffers is an illusion.

SHALAVADI, NEAR POONA, INDIA A unique death tryst spot. This is Ranjit Pardwallah trying to commit ritual suicide. As you can see he is in the middle of three levels of railway lines: the one below is for the lower caste, and the one above for the very high caste; he is middle caste. Alas the trains are very infrequent; this is the fifty-sixth day of his suicide, and he is now suffering from starvation. The story has it that he caught flu, and died in Poona Hospital, egged on by Mother Theresa.

OTTIKUMAND, INDIA A sensation in its day. A Colonel Barrington-Twat, who died abruptly of Tigers, had left wishes that he should be buried on a hill, but on reaching the top he suddenly burst up from his coffin and announced that he was still alive.

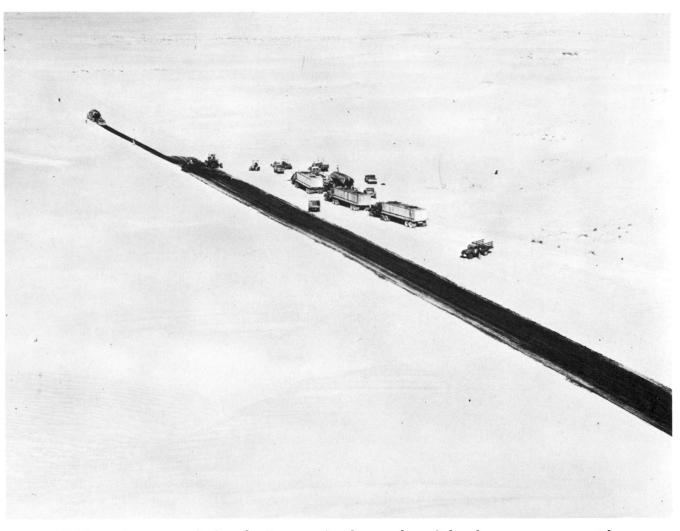

UNO workmen repainting the Equator in places where it has been worn away. The United Nations spend up to £2 million a year on this work.

Korean coolies transporting secret Arthur Scargill Miners' Funds to a less detectable bank in Outer Mongolia.

**PARIS, FRANCE M. Louis Vallon nearing the
eighteenth mile of his attempt to take off
and fly. To date he has run 600 miles
in attempted take-offs.**

GREAT VICTORIAN MISTAKES This is the Ilfracombe Life Boat. It was to be launched by Mr Robert Sprotts (standing with white beard) when it was discovered that they had forgotten to make the oars, so instead the boat was mounted on wheels and pulled around the town with the crew singing 'Sailors of the Queen', and Mr Sprotts reading excerpts from *Sea Tales*, by Mrs Bullington-Quot.

Ken Livingstone in a desperate attempt to sell himself to the electorate.

A deranged Australian trying to hold up a road sign.

A THEATRICAL DISASTER, TRANSVAAL, SOUTH AFRICA The Cinderella story was marred when people employed a second-class fairy godmother to wave her wand over the mice and the pumpkin. This is what happened; Cinderella is the one without the beard.

FLORENCE, ITALY A dead topiary hedge being taken away for burial.

**KWAZULU, SOUTH AFRICA A flying saucer landing near Catford,
complete with Martian crew.**

PONGOLAND, AFRICA Early photo showing missionaries teaching the natives 'Ring-a-ring-a-roses'. They are just reaching the 'a-tishoo, a-tishoo, we all fall down' part.

Scotsmen from the Northern Scots Isles of Muck sailed this boat with their local phone box 600 miles down the coast to Southend to reduce the price of a telephone call to London.

THE CLASS WAR Early British tramcars, showing the upper and lower classes.

MUGINDI, AUSTRALIA Shows the mud-making plant. This plant mixes over a million tons of earth with a million gallons of water each month. The mud is exported to countries which don't have any, or use it to throw at people.

**The winning entry in the 'Build a Hearse for Mrs Thatcher' contest.
The winner comes from Catford.**

**DURBAN, NATAL Bullocks towing away the remains of the British Lions Rugby Team
after their disastrous 1983 tour.**

SMOLENSK, RUSSIA Serge Disterin with his brilliant innovation of making aeroplanes safer to fly in by keeping them on rails.

SHATT EL ARRAB, MESOPOTAMIA Captain Gerald Nitts, awaiting new legs for his camel before setting off in search of the source of the Tigris.

**BROCKLEY, LONDON Dick and Len Frocks,
two brothers who used this effort in an
attempt to avoid conscription in the
Second World War.**